Summary of

Blue Ocean Strategy

How to Create Uncontested Market Space and
Make the Competition Irrelevant

by W. Chan Kim and Renée A. Mauborgne

Instaread

Please Note

This is a summary with analysis.

Table of Contents

Overview

Blue Ocean Strategy, Expanded Edition: How to Create Uncontested Market Space and Make the Competition Irrelevant is the 2015 update to the classic business strategy text of the same name originally published in 2005. The text offers a practical handbook to business students and entrepreneurs who wish to rise above the fray of the competition, become pioneers in previously uncharted market territory, and gain access to impressive growth opportunities and an untapped customer base.

Most businesses make the mistake of focusing on their competitors when developing strategies. A "blue ocean" business, on the other hand, focuses on how to create new value for customers, the base of which may be people who are not yet customers of this business' core industry. The term "blue ocean" is derived from the idea that an area of unexplored market space is like the clear, blue waters of an undisturbed portion of ocean. The opposite of the blue ocean would be the "red ocean," where excessive competition has churned the waters bloody with rivalry.

Simply creating a new product or service is not enough. It is vital to the success and growth of the would-be blue ocean company that it innovate a concept that is useful to the consumer, target-priced for maximum profitability, and able to be executed without encountering resistance or confusion from all involved. Even then, however, blue ocean entrepreneurs cannot rest on their laurels. No industry and no company can survive off the success of a single idea. Instead, the blue ocean entrepreneur must constantly seek new areas in which to innovate and grow.

Important People

W. Chan Kim is the co-author of *Blue Ocean Strategy*. He is the co-director of the Blue Ocean Strategy Institute at INSEAD, an international business school, as well as a fellow of the World Economic Forum.

Renée A. Mauborgne is the co-author of *Blue Ocean Strategy* and is the co-director of the Blue Ocean Strategy Institute at INSEAD. She is also a fellow of the World Economic Forum and is a member of President Barack Obama's Board of Advisors on Historically Black Colleges and Universities.

Guy Laliberté is the CEO of Cirque du Soleil. He created an entirely new type of entertainment experience for people who were never customers of traditional circuses.

William Bratton was the commissioner of the NYPD from 1994 to 1996 and from 2014 to 2016. He is an example of an effective blue ocean strategist who was able to overhaul the New York City police force during his first tenure as commissioner.

Key Takeaways

1. The blue ocean strategy empowers organizations to create entirely new markets for themselves instead of battling competitors in increasingly crowded territory.

2. A red ocean business typically focuses its strategy on beating the competition.

3. When creating a blue ocean strategy, decision makers must consider four questions, each relating to improvements or eliminations that can be made in comparison to others in the industry.

4. Blue ocean businesses do not allow themselves to be stymied by industry conventions and structure.

5. Execution is critical to a successful blue ocean strategy.

6. A blue ocean strategy can only be successful when optimized for profitability.

7. Good blue ocean leaders are able to overcome the main obstacles to execution inside their organization.

8. The ability to construct a blue ocean strategy has never been more important than it is now

because users and consumers are increasingly causing industries to shift and change.

9. No company can permanently remain in the blue ocean without renewing and revising its long-term vision.

Thank you for purchasing this Instaread book

**Download the Instaread mobile app to get
unlimited text & audio summaries
of bestselling books.**

Visit Instaread.co
to learn more.

Analysis

Key Takeaway 1

The blue ocean strategy empowers organizations to create entirely new markets for themselves instead of battling competitors in increasingly crowded territory.

Analysis

Developing new and previously unforeseen value is at the heart of building a blue ocean business because it involves innovating new market space instead of fighting the same old battles with competitors. A blue ocean business is successful when the company can ensure that the price, usefulness, and relative cost of its product or service all are in alignment. To align these factors, a blue ocean company must have a total, systematic, and holistic approach to keeping its own costs down and enhancing consumer value while creating the highest possible number of opportunities and allowing the lowest possible number of risks. Not every company needs to be a blue ocean company; there will always be some value in being the best amid a field of competitors.

Tesla Motors is a prime example of a blue ocean business. In 2003, rather than attempt to beat the large, well-established automakers including Ford, GM, and Chrysler, Tesla co-founder and CEO Elon Musk chose to develop value in an entirely innovative area, electric vehicles, where the competition had yet to wholeheartedly invest. At that time, most car companies built electric and hybrid vehicles to be what the industry calls "compliance cars" developed merely to satisfy government regulations that they invest in green technologies as opposed to vehicles that are designed to arouse consumer interest. Tesla, although not the first company to build electric vehicles, was the first to build one that satisfied a desire for a zero-emissions car while generating aesthetic appeal and harnessing the allure of a sports car. In fact, the Tesla has outperformed its gas-guzzling competitors; it has demonstrated speedier acceleration than Ferrari, Lamborghini, and Bugatti in 2015 road tests. [1]

Key Takeaway 2

A red ocean business typically focuses its strategy on beating the competition.

Analysis

When a business invests too many of its strategic efforts into beating the competition, it often begins to resemble its rivals in spite of itself. A blue ocean company simply renders the competition obsolete, redundant, or otherwise irrelevant. Unlike a red ocean business, blue ocean organizations are able to successfully rebuild and transcend the previously accepted boundaries of their market to escape the competition. In order to do so, the company's decision makers should examine the typical alternatives to their industry that consumers are choosing—and determine when and why these alternatives are sought. Blue ocean leaders can position their company to face a different set of consumers or clients; for example, to shift from being a business-facing company to being a consumer-facing company. They can also examine current industry trends to try to find hints of future preferences and habits already being expressed by some consumers.

When Zocdoc, an online doctor's appointment scheduling company, first launched in 2007, there were plenty of computer software systems competing for medical facilities to use for their internal scheduling services. At the time, however, none of these services were consumer-facing, which meant patients still had to call doctors' offices and attempt to negotiate for an available appointment. This longstanding method of scheduling medical appointments left patients largely unable to know if another doctor in the same specialty might be able to see them sooner.

Rather than take the red ocean strategy of trying to improve upon the services offered by existing scheduling tools for doctors' offices, Zocdoc transformed the business model to position these scheduling services directly to the consumer. Instead of putting the power in the hands of a receptionist in a clinic, prospective patients could now make their own appointments online without ever picking up the phone. This shift marked Zocdoc's entrance into blue ocean territory; it positioned itself to a new audience and left behind competitors in the medical scheduling software business. In so doing, it created new and previously unforeseen value and demand. As of 2015, Zocdoc is worth $1.8 billion and doctors' offices now pay to be listed on the company's app. [2]

Key Takeaway 3

When creating a blue ocean strategy, decision makers must consider four questions, each relating to improvements or eliminations that can be made in comparison to others in the industry.

Analysis

Developing a blue ocean strategy means determining what to scrap and what to salvage from an existing industry in order to forge new territory. Decision makers must ask themselves questions to determine which industry elements can be dropped, which can be implemented below current industry standards, which can be improved beyond current industry standards, and what new standards or features can transform the industry. These four general questions can help guide the team to build the best possible strategy.

For example, if Peg is an entrepreneur who wants to launch a doggie daycare service that deploys a blue ocean strategy, she may begin by looking at which parts of the industry can be tossed and, in doing so, drive down costs without sacrificing utility or value. Perhaps most doggie daycare facilities retain an in-house groomer. Skilled groomers can be expensive to keep on staff because they often require extensive training in methods of cutting fur, trimming nails, and other services. Realizing this, Peg might make some inquiries and find that most customers only need their dogs bathed and brushed but not fully groomed. Many, in fact, prefer one of the specialty groomers in her city. As a result, she may choose to eliminate this typically standard service in favor of a minimum-wage employee who can bathe and brush any dog when needed and then help in another area of the business when no dogs need bathing.

Next, Peg might consider which industry standards can be delivered better and which can be delivered to a lesser extent without losing ground to the competition. Perhaps she finds that, while it is a nice amenity, most owners don't read their dogs' daily report cards. So she might dial back to using a live cam in the area where the dogs play with each other. After some initial success, she might notice that her competitors use doggie cams of rather poor image quality and resolution—so she might install a higher-resolution system that owners can truly enjoy while away from their pets. Lastly, Peg realizes that many dog owners are commuters who don't use a daycare service because it's more convenient to have a dog walker come to their home during the day and walk their pooch privately. However, the costs are higher for these private services and the dogs lack social interaction with other pooches. Peg realizes she can tap this audience if she can provide an on-demand pick-up time for dogs—something no other doggie daycare in town provides. Soon, Peg finds herself in blue ocean territory when her daycare launches an app for on-demand doggie pick-ups that utilize existing car-hailing services in her city.

Key Takeaway 4

Blue ocean businesses do not allow themselves to be stymied by industry conventions and structure.

Analysis

Blue ocean organizations reinvent the industries in which they exist. They do not fall into the typical industry trap of focusing only on existing customers. Instead, these businesses understand that non-customers are often the best place to find what the company should be offering if it wants to tap new demand instead of attempting to stir up interest from the same customer base as the rest of its competitors. To stay out of typical industry battles, blue ocean strategies do not get overly entangled in the day-to-day numbers.

For years, animal shelters have been overcrowded with cats and dogs. Would-be owners, however, continued to buy animals from pet shops when perfectly good ones could be obtained for a small fee from a local rescue. Despite shelter efforts to bring prospective pet owners in the doors, many were turned off by the look, feel, and even smell of these places; the animals in pet stores appeared in a more familiar and friendly retail environment. Petfinder.com, however, broke free of the industry mold by taking the shelter system online. On the site, prospective pet adopters can search a database of adoptable pets in their area through an interface that is very similar to most dating websites and features the animals' names and bios. This site removed the obstacle that typically stood between prospective owners and homeless pets waiting to be adopted. In this way, Petfinder.com looked at the industry's non-customers and found a way to engage them in a comfortable, online setting.

Key Takeaway 5

Execution is critical to a successful blue ocean strategy.

Analysis

If a blue ocean strategy cannot be executed, it is without merit. When a company pursues one of these strategies, all parties involved must be able to understand the new direction and describe it for themselves in clear, simple terms. The company should never attempt to keep these strategic changes secret from its own personnel.

Visualization is an important tool for building understanding on the road to execution. A company may wish to provide employees with a simple graph demonstrating the value curve that the new, blue ocean strategy will enact. Through clear communication with employees, partners, and the public, a company can ensure that there is no effort to sabotage or resist change on the road to execution.

Studies have repeatedly shown that visual learning can lead to better fact retention and comprehension than verbal explanations alone. Most recently, a 2015 study from Washington University found that when college students were provided a diagram or illustration ahead of a science lecture, they were better able to engage with the subject matter and process it on a more profound level than test subjects provided only with outlines or the experience of hearing the lecture alone. [3] For a company trying to communicate the path to executing a new vision, employing simple but effective visuals can be much more effective in building stakeholder understanding and buy-in than a staff meeting in which changes are simply described.

Key Takeaway 6

A blue ocean strategy can only be successful when optimized for profitability.

Analysis

A blue ocean business must focus first and foremost on how useful its offering is for a prospective buyer. A quick trick to ensure that the product is buyer-friendly and easy to understand is to see if a catchy tagline can be devised to sell it. Once the company leaders are certain that their offering has buyer utility, they must set a price for their service or product that will ensure strong margins but remain within the purchasing power of the target consumer.

If a company is unable to define its product with the simplicity of a tagline, its leadership may be trying to develop something that customers will fail to understand and desire. Consider the famous tagline for M&Ms: "The milk chocolate melts in your mouth, not in your hand." Dating back to 1954, this slogan communicated efficiently and effectively that this candy product was not as likely to stain one's hands or clothes as its competitors and could be enjoyed without fear of the elements overheating it while on the go. [4] Another slogan that has stood the test of time thanks to its ability to communicate a product's value proposition to consumers is that of the diamond seller De Beers, which famously began using the now-classic tagline "A Diamond is Forever" in 1948. At the time, diamonds had yet to become culturally linked to engagement and marriage. The slogan was instrumental in communicating that for men looking to promise everlasting love, a diamond was the best way to do it. [5] With its memorable slogan, De Beers was able to tell consumers exactly why they needed to shell out large sums of money for its product.

Key Takeaway 7

Good blue ocean leaders are able to overcome the main obstacles to execution inside of their organization.

Analysis

For a blue ocean business, there are generally four main obstacles to execution: the need to alert employees of the need to change, the fact that resources required for changes may be limited, the lack of motivation from any involved parties, and the internal politics inherent to any organization.

Overcoming obstacles to execution is a critical part of optimizing a blue ocean strategy. A good blue ocean manager is able to make stakeholders want to buy into change of their own free will as opposed to feeling pushed into doing things in an unfamiliar way. These managers are also able to identify key parties within their organizations who will fight for the new strategy—or against it. Armed with that knowledge, a manager will be able to manage these people accordingly. Most importantly, however, blue ocean management ensures that "fair process" is carried out. "Fair process" engages employees, explains the changes at hand, and makes the expectations involved in the shift extremely clear to all involved so that no one feels undermined, confused, or excluded from the process.

Time and again, industry has seen declining employee engagement in the workforce. In many cases, experts attribute this problem to the fact that managers fail to bring employees to the table on decision-making and instead treat their workers as cogs in a machine. [6] Perhaps more dangerous to implementing and executing a blue ocean strategy is that employee disengagement can, in many cases, lead to outright hostility against the organization. [7] By ensuring that "fair process" is carried out, a company leader can overcome three of the four main obstacles to execution.

Key Takeaway 8

The ability to construct a blue ocean strategy has never been more important than it is now because users and consumers are increasingly causing industries to shift and change.

Analysis

Social media has elevated the reach and influence of consumer voices advocating for their own needs and responding to experiences with businesses and products. Furthermore, the expansion of internet communication platforms means that organizations are increasingly forced to consider how they serve a global marketplace as opposed to simply focusing on their local communities.

For decades, businesses and the mainstream media have been able to control the narratives surrounding their brands—both positive and negative. Today, customers are more empowered than ever to deliver their honest and unvarnished opinions about the products and services they encounter. Whether a customer is reviewing a restaurant on Yelp or uploading a video blog on YouTube about whether or not a certain makeup product does everything it promises to do on the label, consumer voices are guiding public perception in unprecedented ways. Because the core goal of any blue ocean strategy is to create new value for consumers, devising a product or service that is able to make consumers sing its praises is more valuable than ever.

Emily Weiss's beauty-brand brainchild, Glossier, is one such example. It was propelled to online dominance by her highly popular blog *Into the Gloss*. After building a cult following of readers who valued her authentic opinion on beauty products, she became a blue ocean entrepreneur in her own right by launching her own line of products targeted for the Instagram generation. Today, her products are routinely sold out and boast lengthy waiting lists. [8]

Key Takeaway 9

No company can permanently remain in the blue ocean without renewing and revising its long-term vision.

Analysis

The process of building a blue ocean company is ongoing and sensitive to the fact that no matter how good its idea, a company will inevitably attract imitators who will try to compete in the new market space it pioneers. It's important to remember that blue ocean businesses are not always the first to market a new offering—they're the first to unite innovation with value and effectively reach consumers.

National Geographic is a strong example of a company that has constantly embraced change and renewal to remain in the blue ocean for more than a century. After publishing its first magazine in 1888, *National Geographic* remained a household and coffee table staple for decades as customers marveled over its winning visuals. However, by the 1990s, subscription numbers began to take a dive and, like many of its competitors in print media, *National Geographic* appeared to be experiencing its death throes. The company refused to consign itself to print obsolescence and instead launched the National Geographic Channel in 2001. The channel was a pioneer in providing exciting reality television for a television market that was still interested in the medium but worn out on dating and game shows. Even now, the company is undergoing another shift toward embracing higher-end, premium content in a bid to become the HBO of science television. [9]

Author's Style

Kim and Mauborgne write both academically and practically to serve a wide variety of readers in and out of business school classrooms. The text functions as an academic study into business strategies that work and why, but it can also serve as a how-to manual for a business leader hoping to build a blue ocean organization. The text relies heavily on the use of charts and graphs to illustrate where blue ocean businesses have been able to succeed over others in their respective industries. The authors describe how business leaders can develop these charts and graphs for themselves so that they can predict whether or not any particular idea meets the criteria for becoming a successful blue ocean business.

Author's Perspective

Kim and Mauborgne met 30 years ago when Kim was Mauborgne's professor. Since then, the two have pioneered global business strategies that, most famously, included the 2005 publication of *Blue Ocean Strategy*. They bring an academic perspective to their subject matter, such as challenging the conventional wisdom of business strategy by employing a 10-year study of 150 strategic efforts undertaken over the course of a century and across 30 industries. This wide range of data provides the authors with a variety of examples to draw upon when illustrating their suggestions for how to effectively carve out new territory with a blue ocean strategy.

~~~~ END OF INSTAREAD ~~~~

Thank you for purchasing this Instaread book

**Download the Instaread mobile app to get
unlimited text & audio summaries
of bestselling books.**

Visit Instaread.co
to learn more.

References

1. Valdes-Dapena, Peter. "Tesla beats Ferrari, Lamborghini, Bugatti." *CNNMoney.* October 29, 2015. Accessed August 2, 2016. http://money.cnn.com/2015/10/29/autos/tesla-fast/

2. Griffith, Erin. "ZocDoc lands unicorn valuation." *Fortune.* August 20, 2015. Accessed August 2, 2016. http://fortune.com/2015/08/20/zocdoc-unicorn-valuation/

3. Bui, Dung C., and Mark A. McDaniel. "Enhancing learning during lecture note-taking using outlines and illustrative diagrams." *Journal of Applied Research in Memory and Cognition* 4, no. 2 (June 2015): 129-35. http://www.sciencedirect.com/science/article/pii/S2211368115000200

4. Schultz, E.J. "Rewind: 1954 Ad Shows M&Ms Characters Go for a Chocolatey Swim." *Advertising Age.* May 9, 2013. Accessed August 2, 2016. http://adage.com/article/rewind/1954-ad-shows-m-ms-characters-a-chocolatey-swim/241375/

5. Sullivan, J. Courtney. "Why 'A Diamond Is Forever' has lasted so long." *Washington Post.* February 7, 2014. Accessed August 2, 2016. https://www.washingtonpost.com/opinions/why-a-diamond-is-forever-has-lasted-so-long/2014/02/07/f6adf3f4-8eae-11e3-84e1-27626c5ef5fb_story.html

6. Morgan, Jacob. "This Is The Single Greatest Cause Of Employee Disengagement." *Forbes.* October 13, 2014. Accessed August 2, 2016. http://www.forbes.com/sites/jacobmorgan/2014/10/13/this-is-the-single-greatest-cause-of-employee-disengagement/#76c4094f211d

7. David, Susan. "Disengaged Employees? Do Something About It." *Harvard Business Review.* July 15, 2013. Accessed August 2, 2016. https://hbr.org/2013/07/disengaged-employees-do-someth

8. O'Connor, Clare. "How Glossier's Emily Weiss Is Using The Internet To Build A Beauty Brand For Generation Instagram." *Forbes.* August 2, 2016. Accessed August 2, 2016. http://www.forbes.com/sites/clareoconnor/2016/08/02/how-glossiers-emily-weiss-is-using-the-internet-to-build-a-beauty-brand-for-generation-instagram/#74a27ef04117

9. Gillette, Felix. "Inside National Geographic's HBO-Inspired Murdoch Makeover." *Bloomberg.com.* May 17, 2016. Accessed August 2, 2016. http://www.bloomberg.com/news/features/2016-05-17/inside-national-geographic-s-hbo-inspired-murdoch-makeover